Historic Walks around the West Pennine Moors

John Dixon & Jaana Järvinen

Historic Walks around the West Pennine Moors
by John Dixon and Jaana Järvinen

Copyright © John Dixon and Jaana Järvinen, 1988

Published by Carnegie Press, 125 Woodplumpton Road, Cadley, Preston PR2 2LS

Typeset and Printed by T. Snape & Co. Ltd., Bolton's Court, Preston

First edition, September 1988

ISBN 0 948789 20 4

Contents

Introduction		5
Walk 1	— The Ancients Look Down	6
Walk 2	— The Stones of Ice and Men	15
Walk 3	— Crucks and Castles	24
Walk 4	— Old homesteads around the Roman way	33
Walk 5	— Oak Valley traverse	40
Walk 6	— Livesey-cum-Tockholes	53

The sketch maps in this book are intended to indicate the route in a general way. Walkers should use the O.S. Pathfinder maps to locate the exact routes.

Introduction

The West Pennine Moors are those high open spaces of moorland, valleys and reservoirs which rise above the mill towns of Darwen, Bolton and Greater Manchester. The high moors can seem bleak and forbidding on an overcast day, but on a clear day they attract one like a magnet, to wander the moors seemingly for ever. The moors are marked by man's settlement and activity by features which go back many thousands of years. Traces of early man's endeavours can be seen throughout the area. Their tombs, homesteads and stone monuments point to the existence of a stable and settled community in those times. It has often been thought that early Lancashire was 'backward', thinly populated, somehow less civilised than other more southerly parts of the country. Archaeology has been a relatively neglected pastime in the county and, because of this, not much is known for certain about the distant past in Lancashire. However, discoveries are being made all the time and, with each new find, our knowledge increases. As the area covered by this book testifies, even the casual observer can find traces of man's early history. With a little more research, and a little more funding for archaeology, it might well be that the whole notion of Lancashire being 'backward' will need to be reconsidered.

Today's harsh climate and poor soils support sparse grasses, on which sheep and some cattle graze. Many of the old sheep farms are long gone, remembered only by the low walls of their ruins. These farmers often supported their families by having other jobs. Small quarries provided stone for walls, buildings and millstones, the rough gritty rock being good for grinding corn. The hill-folk also spun, wove and bleached wool, from which skills and ideas grew, eventually feeding and supporting the Industrial Revolution. As our towns grew, their way of life changed drastically, part of their lands giving way to the vast new reservoirs needed to provide the lifeblood and energy reserves for new enterprise. Years later, the sons and daughters of those early mill-folk have once again returned to the hills and moors, not to farm and toil with stone, but to relax and freely stroll in the good clean air. For a small time the pace of modern life is forgotten as the near landscape draws us in.

The walks described here are more rambles of exploration and are designed to give the native and visitor alike a greater awareness of man's role in the development of these uplands. Let the moorland walk be a time for reflection, to learn to know where you are now and where you came from. Enjoy the hills which have for so long been so closely a part of the lives, economies and culture of the people of the West Pennines.

Walk One

The Ancients Look Down

9 & 5 miles, 6 & 3 hours respectively

Use O.S. Pathfinder Maps SD 62/72 & 61/71

This walk climbs steeply from the village of Brinscall and skirts Brown Hill to enter the enchanted valley of Dean Black. On the distant skyline Round Loaf invites us and, on ascending Black Hill, the views one gets from this friendly mound are magnificent, even though the peat blanket hides its ancient secrets. On past the old lead workings to view Lancashire's most ancient monument, the first known resting place of a man in the region. From the moorland heights we quickly descend into a rolling green and rural landscape which culminates in the tranquil beauty of the tiny hamlet of White Coppice. On a summer's day, the lark's song is only broken by the sound of leather on willow. We leave this paradise behind us to wend our way through leafy lanes, long ago abandoned by the rustic traffic, to reach the water's edge and Brinscall once again.

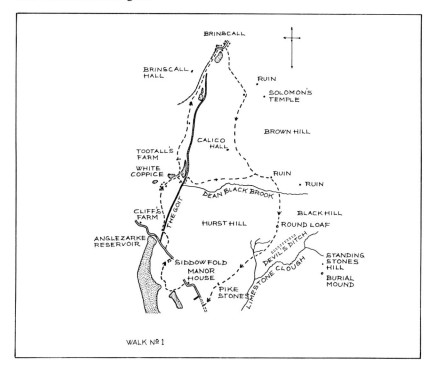

WALK Nº 1

As can be seen from the map, this ramble can be taken as one or two shorter walks. For the long walk we suggest Brinscall as your starting point; for the two shorter ones, White Coppice.

Brinscall to Round Loaf

From the bottom of School Lane cross the 'Goit' to bend right and climb the old lane leading to the moors. Follow trackway up to go over a stile in fence by a ruin. Follow right-hand trackway along the moor to a footpath sign. Walk on, past the ruin, to follow the field down to the stream. Cross the stream and walk directly up to Round Loaf.

Round Loaf Tumulus

Round Loaf is the local name given to the round cairn or bowl barrow which stands in a conspicuous position on the side of Black Hill Upper. The mound is slightly elongated, measuring about 50 metres north-south and 45 metres east-west. In the summit of the mound is a small disturbance hollow caused by local 'flint' seekers. Now that the site is a Scheduled Ancient Monument it is hoped that this type of robbery will cease. The mound shows no traces of an outer ditch, which has led some to suggest that the mound was actually formed by the action of a glacier during the last Ice Age. Only further archaeological investigation will determine the true nature of the mound. Whatever the origin of the cairn, it provides a good resting spot giving excellent views of the surrounding moorland landscape.

Devil's Ditch

Devil's Ditch was constructed in the 18th century as part of the lead mining complex on Anglezarke Moor. Its purpose was to give a greater force of water to Limestone Brook which fed the waterwheel pit further down Limestone Clough. The earliest record of lead mining on Anglezarke is from 1692 when Sir Richard Standish of Duxbury, the then landowner, signed an agreement with Peter Shaw of Rivington and others to extract and process the lead ore. The mines were worked off and on until 1837, from which time they fell into ruin. The shafts were filled in the 1930s to provide work for the unemployed people of Chorley. Since 1982 some of the remaining features, the slime and waterwheel pits, have been partially excavated by today's unemployed under the direction of various government agencies.

Round Loaf to Pikestones

Follow the path from Round Loaf, keeping Rivington Pike on your left, down to the stream. Follow the stream down to the edge of the plantation. Follow the top edge of the plantation, along the contour, to Pikestones.

THE PIKESTONES

The Pikestones, Anglezarke   NGR 627172

'The Pikestones' is the local name given to a group of stones on Anglezarke Moor which are in fact the remains of a Megalithic chambered tomb, the only one known to exist in Lancashire. Today, this badly robbed and ruined long cairn consists of the remains of a rectangular chamber, possibly divided into two compartments set towards the northern end of an elongated cairn of small stones and partly covered with peat and grass. The alignment is north-south, measuring about 150 feet long, 62 feet wide at the northern end and 45 feet at the southern end. There is no retaining kerb but some of the perimeter stones are somewhat larger than the stones of the cairn. Of the chamber itself two stones at the eastern end remain upright and a west side-stone leans against them. Behind these are two fallen stones which were once a roof stone and a back stone respectively, the latter having fallen outwards. Three small stones are set across the northern end and it has been suggested that these may have acted as a sill dividing the 14-foot long chamber into two.

The true ground plan of the Pikestones has been the subject of two archaeological surveys: Dr. J. D. Bullock *(TLCAS.* Vol. LXVIII. 1958) and Frances Lynch *(PPS.* Vol. XXXII. 1966) respectively. Both survey drawings are reproduced here, but I consider that each falls short of the true form and present layout of the monument. I take this view from my own close inspection of the site which has shown inconsistencies and omissions in both surveys. What is needed is a systematic geophysical survey and an analysis of the computer data – a worthwhile task for the newly formed Central Lancashire Archaeological Research Unit.

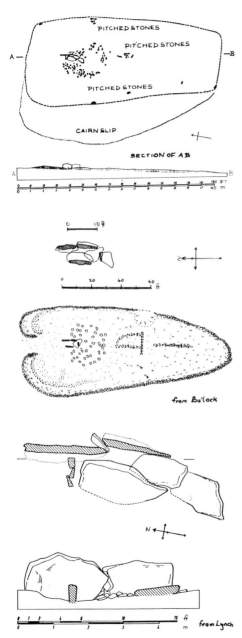

This Megalithic structure represents the product of a high point in Neolithic society in Lancashire. The building of such a large monument would have consumed an appreciable share of the community's time, energy and effort. Its construction and use would to some extent have performed a communal function, although it was probably directed by and for a small elite. The tomb is built on the edge of the then settled landscape – the Lancashire Neolithic Floor. The 'floor' is today preserved in the peat deposits of our upland moors. The mean temperature was 2°C higher than it is today, which allowed farming and settlement to exist at far higher elevations than today. It is usually thought that they worked the lighter, higher soils as they did not have the technological force to exploit and clear the dense forests or till the heavy clay of the poorly drained valley floors, although recent practical experiments, in Scandinavia and elsewhere, have suggested that the humble stone axe, which is found in large numbers throughout the country, was a formidable tool which was capable of felling even fairly substantial hardwoods. As the climate became cooler and wetter, in combination with the artificial clearance of forest in the upland areas which led to a gradual leaching of soil nutrients, sphagnum moss and cotton grass colonized the uplands resulting in the blanket of peat bog which is so widespread today. This combination of factors led Neolithic man from his upland settlements down to the lower levels, a process which would only become complete in the Late Bronze Age.

This type of tomb does not represent the burial site of only one person but of many persons over a period of time, and not always the full skeleton was interred in the chamber. Evidence from other sites shows four major patterns: contrasts between articulated and disarticulated skeletons; others between immature and adult individuals; different treatment of male and female burials and a distinction between the left- and right-hand sides of the body. Some have suggested that these arrangements are an assertion of the collective and a denial of the individual and of difference between individuals. An interesting theory, but I think that the true reason for such arrangements lies in the ways that bodies were stripped of flesh in the mortuary enclosures.

Many other chambered tombs await discovery in the Lancashire region and probable structures have been located in the Bowland and Rossendale districts. If all or most of the Megalithic structures could be located in the region we may then gain some knowledge of territorial divisions in Neolithic times. It is conceivable that in Lancashire a particular form of agriculture was practised – the village might be found to have remained in one place for a decade or so and, then, as the land nearby became exhausted, move on to new land in the same territory. The tomb, or some other monument, would provide a territorial focal point for that family group, an enduring symbol of the continuity of their occupation of the land. Each group would probably have consisted of around thirty persons – a single farming family, belonging to a larger folk/clan spread throughout the region, each group holding one territory, served by one tomb.

The building of Pikestones would have taken the twenty or so able-bodied inhabitants of 'Anglezarke Territory' over thirty days. Such an investment of labour would have to be made over a number of years, and at times when there was little farming activity. It is reasonable to suppose that they may have called upon the help of other neighbouring groups to join in the construction work.

Pikestones to Manor House

Walk down along the edge of plantation to go over a fence (there should be a stile here) and over a stile by a gate. Turn right and walk along the lane to go through a gate. Walk down the road. Manor House is the first house on the right.

MANOR HOUSE

Manor House

Manor House, or High Bullough as it was once known, stands on a commanding position aside the Anglezarke road. The house bears three date stones, 1604 R.S., 1620 and 1779, the first of these relating to the Shaw family. John Shaw of High Bullough was a great benefactor of Rivington Church, where his name appears on a memorial brass.

Manor House to Siddow Fold

Go through the kissing-gate by the road in front of the house. Cross field directly to go through a gate. Follow path down to go over a footbridge and on, past another footbridge (do not go over) to turn right at crossing pathways. Follow path to go over a stile, on, over a footbridge and on, to turn right by a clough filled in with gravel stone. Walk up along the clough to go through a gate. Follow right-hand fence to go through a gate onto road. Siddow Fold is on the right.

SIDDOW FOLD

Siddow Fold

Siddow Fold, now named Gamekeeper's Cottage, is an attractive Jacobean cottage with a fine whitewashed front. The door lintel bears the date 1707 with the initials I.N., those of John Newton, a preacher at Rivington.

Siddow Fold to White Coppice

Walk down the road to go through a gate on the right. (If you wish to visit Cliff's Farm, continue along the road to the first house on the right). Follow track to go over a stile and a bridge on the left. Follow right-hand wall to go over a stile. Walk up the field on a slight left diagonal to go over a stile by a gate. Follow left-hand wall to go over a stile. Follow trackway to White Coppice Farm. Walk down the farmlane to turn left into White Coppice.

Cliff's Farm

With round-headed and straight-headed windows to the front, Cliff's presents an interesting face to the inquiring eye. The farm is dated 1696, with the initials T.A. & R.M. with a single M above.

White Coppice

The tiny hamlet of White Coppice grew up around Alfred Eccles' weaving mill. The mill has long been demolished; all that remains of it today is the lodge, now a favourite haunt of fishermen. Eccles was a firm advocate of temperance in drinking and smoking and devoted much energy and wealth to its advancement. Even today there is no watering hole in the village.

There are many 18th-century cottages to be found in the village, those in The Row being good examples. What was once the village green is now a most picturesque cricket field, and on a lazy summer's day it is a favourite picnic spot with room for children to play amid delightful surroundings.

White Coppice to Tootall's Farm

Walk back to White Coppice Farm, past the house and on along the lane to the cricket field. Turn left at corner of a small white cottage and follow path up to go over a stile in fence, then through a gate opposite to enter Tootall's Farm.

WHITE COPPICE

Tootall's Farm to Brinscall

Walk past the house, turn right and follow path to go over a stile. Follow old trackway to go over a stile. Cross field on a right diagonal to a corner in fences. Follow left-hand fence to go through a gate onto lane. Follow lane down to go through a kissing-gate opposite. Cross field directly to go over a stile. Walk straight on to go over a stile and a footbridge. Cross field on a right diagonal to far corner to go over a stile. Follow path onto a lane. Walk along the lane to Brinscall.

Brinscall

Brinscall is first mentioned in 1200, then named Brendescoles, meaning 'the burnt huts'. Why the huts were burnt is lost to the record of pre-history; all we can be sure of from the name is that it must have once been a Scandinavian settlement some time before the Norman Conquest. During the 10th century, Norse farmers settled on the marginal lands on the edges of the old shires of Leyland, Blackburn and Amounderness.

Today the once thriving weaving village is fading back into the surrounding rural landscape. Little moves apart from strollers around the water's edge, the railway has been and gone and only the ducks remain to break the peace of a Sunday afternoon.

Walk Two

The Stones of Ice and Men

12 miles, 8 hours, plus lunch

Use Map O.S. SD61/71 Pathfinder Series

For those with a love of wild moorland, broken only by sheets of clear blue waters, this walk offers many pleasures. The retreating ice has carved massive hillside formations like the hanging stones and fortress type structures we see on Andrew's Buttery and above Green Lowe. Man too has left his mark with stones in the form of circles and ring-bank cairns established in the Bronze Age, and the gritstone farmsteads of a later age that now lie derelict across the moors. This walk explores man's life and environment on these windswept hilltops from early times to the present day, taking in a wide variety of places of interest. For lunch we recommend the Cross Guns Inn at Dimple, where good food is served at very reasonable prices. But don't feast too well, for you've Turton Heights in front of you.

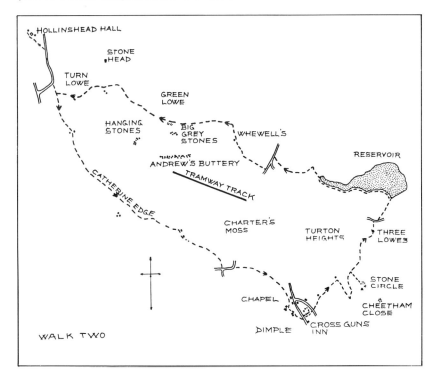

Hollinshead Hall

In the early 1200s the manor of Tockholes, in the township of Livesey, was in the possession of a branch of the de Pleasington family who took the local name as their surname. The de Tocholes were later followed by the Radcliffes of Ordall who had their manor house on the site of Lower Hill cottages. They held the manor until 1641 when it was sold. Part of the manor, the Hollinshead, was purchased by Edward Warren who built a large yeoman farmhouse there. In 1666 he was assessed for tax on eight hearths in his properties there. Some time after 1761 the house and lands were sold to John Hollinshead. Being in a ruinous condition at that time, the house was for the most part demolished and rebuilt in 1776. The Well House was also built at this time, replacing the old farm well. Upon the death of John Hollinshead, the estate descended to his cousin William Brock, who assumed the additional name of Hollinshead. In 1803 the estate passed to his nephew Lawrence Brock, who also assumed the additional surname of Hollinshead. He sold the manor of Hollinshead to Eccles Shorrock, a Blackburn merchant and mill owner. The Hall was abandoned and demolished when Liverpool Waterworks acquired the lands for water catchment.

Recently the site of the 18th-century hall and farm has been tidied up as part of a government aided scheme. The aim is to transform the site into an area for public recreation, incorporating the feature into the Roddleworth Nature Trail. With the old well still, for the most part, in its original state and the ground plan of the buildings discernible by the low walls, the project should prove to be a most worthwhile venture.

The pathway that we take from the site of the hall follows the line of the pre-turnpike road which ran from Wood Fold, through Hollinshead and along Catherine Edge, to Longworth Hall and Dimple.

HOLLINSHEAD WELL

Hollinshead Hall to Dimple Chapel

Follow the woodside path from the hall to the roadway. Turn right and follow roadway on to go over stile by gate at road corner. Follow the trackway to distant farm. Walk through the deserted farmyard and follow trackway on for two miles to pass over stile at corner of pine wood. Follow trackway down to the roadway. Turn left and walk down the road to pass through gate on the right. Follow path down to go over footbridge. Right, and follow fenceline up, on, following path to go over stile into wood. Follow path on through the wood to go over stile by gate. Follow trackway on and over stile by gate. Then go right, down to terraced street. Walk along the cobbled street to go between the old gate posts onto trackway, through the iron gate and on down to go through stile by gate to the churchyard.

Charters Moss

Peat digging on the moss has revealed many Bronze Age finds, the best

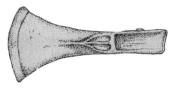

examples being a perforated stone hammer and a bronze palstave (pictured here). Other finds in the area have been a looped socketed spearhead with part of its original wooden shaft, a more developed palstave with improved handle, and a loop-headed spearhead of bronze. All the items display a high standard of workmanship in their manufacture, suggesting a well developed and prosperous community living in the area.

Walmsley Chapel, Dimple

The Walmsley Unitarian Chapel stands near the Walmsley School of 1851 in an isolated spot away from the busy main road. The chapel was built in 1713 and must be one of the oldest of its type in the district. The front is altered from the original. The sides, however, are original, having two tiers of small three-light mullioned windows. Inside are box pews and a pulpit from the early 18th century. The chapel originally stood on the old Egerton Road, now the back road. Its site can still be seen today on the edge of the new estate at the top of the brookside path we take past the estate, on the right.

On our way to the Cross Guns we shall pass Howarths Farm, and a close inspection will reveal some of its 17th-century features.

Unitarian Chapel to Cross Guns Inn

On coming out of front church gates turn right and walk down a few yards to go over old stile on left. Follow right-hand fence to building, left, and walk around the building to the front of the farm (notice the row of mullioned windows on the first foor). Follow farm lane to road. Turn right and walk down to the Cross Guns.

Cross Guns to Dimple Hall

Walk back up the road to turn right into grassed trackway on edge of new estate. Follow path up to the roadway. Cross the road to go over stile opposite. Walk up

the field on a left diagonal to gateway and on to Dimple Hall.

Dimple Hall

Dimple Hall is a mid-Victorian house done in the Gothic revival style. The datestone bears the Initials P.H.A. with a date of 1855. With its open gallery and cross windows it creates a most pleasing picture.

Dimple Hall to stone circles

Walk up the farm lane to enter High Lands yard. Go through stile opposite and follow old trackway up to trees. Turn right and follow track on, over broken wall, to gate-stile (do not go over). Turn around and follow track by wall up the hillside to corner and on, following pathway, to go through old narrow gateway in wall. Follow path on to 'white pole'. Turn right and follow old field boundary to go over stile at wall. Walk on up to the circles.

Cheetham Close stone circle complex

Situated on the bleak moorland plateau of Cheetham Close, above Turton, stands an early Bronze Age village and burial complex. It consists of a stone circle with at least two outliers, two ring-bank cairns and two small cairns of unknown structure. The stone circle is now in a ruinous condition. Ten stones originally formed the circle and though many have been broken and displaced it is still possible to discern the original settings. At a distance of feet south-west from the circle stands a solitary stone 19 inches high, and south-south-east at a distance of 102 feet another outlier can be found.

The ring-bank cairn is located just south of the stone circle, on slightly higher ground. Its circular shape is defined by a low, round rubble and earth bank. When excavated in 1893 it was claimed that the bank was faced both

STONE CIRCLE, TURTON

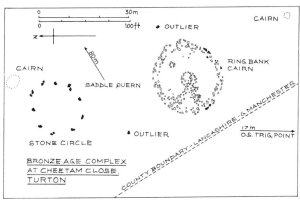

CAIRN

OUTLIER

RING BANK
CAIRN

CAIRN

SADDLE QUERN

OUTLIER

STONE CIRCLE

O.S. TRIG. POINT
17m

COUNTY BOUNDARY - LANCASHIRE - G. MANCHESTER

BRONZE AGE COMPLEX
AT CHEETAM CLOSE,
TURTON

externally and internally by large gritstone slabs set continuously in a kerb. A possible entrance exists on the north east, where a gap about 1m wide is flanked by much thicker sections of bank. In the centre is a low cairn, not clearly defined on the west, and partially destroyed by illicit excavators. A small satellite cairn, 2m in diameter, lies in this north-east quadrant. Two other small cairns lie to the north east and to the south east of the stone circle and ring-bank cairn respectively.

Another ring-bank cairn has been located 700m south east of the triangulation pillar. It is partially overlain by a stone wall and is in a ruinous condition, yet sections of the massive rubble kerb can be distinguished and a large earthfast boulder near the centre may be an integral feature.

In 1954 a Bronze Age saddle quern was found 80m north east of the stone circle. Saddle querns were used for grinding cereal grains into a rough flour. Three barbed-and-tanged arrowheads were also found.

For most of the above information we are indebted to M. Fletcher for his survey work on the above sites.

Much controversy exists as to the function of such stone circles and cairns, with theories ranging from ancient temples to agrarian calendars. However, it is now thought that these complexes represent contemporary sites for ritual and burial respectively, yet even this theory can only explain a part of their role and function. More co-operation between disciplines is needed

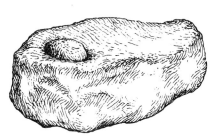

SADDLE QUERN.

to understand their true nature fully and our starting point must be the first permanent settlements in such places as Turton Heights. Before the forest clearance down to the valley floors during the middle to later Bronze Age, which brought soil erosion and impoverishment to the Pennine uplands, such highland sites would have been viable. On looking north from the cairn it is not hard to imagine cultivated fields stretching across the plateau – the finding of the saddle quern testifies to such activity in close proximity to the circles. What then of the circles themselves? First let us look at the structure referred to as a ring-bank cairn. When excavated, the majority of such sites yield many urn-burial cremations. This fact has led many archaeologists to interpret the site solely in terms of a burial complex. If such well-built structures were built for the dead then what fine structures the communities' dwellings must have been, and indeed where are they today? For the answer one must re-examine the ring-bank cairn in wider terms. The cairn itself is simultaneously a place of the living and of the dead. It could well be what remains of a communal living hut with ancestral remains interred beneath the place that was most central to their lives - a well revetted stone-walled building with a turf roof supported by timbers. In the centre of the hut would be a hearth and chimney stack.

We now turn our attention to the stone circle. Again this could be the foundations of a building, but this is doubtful. A more likely explanation is that it is a statement by a social group of the establishment of their territorial rights over an area. A small group of persons squatting on a highland plateau gives no sign to others of permanence – they can easily be displaced. But the erection of a monument which has consumed some communal economic effort implies to others a permanence of settlement, a physical statement that 'We are here, this is ours'. Later such places would gain a symbolic, religious and secular significance – a place of social and economic exchange.

The site at Cheetham Close may have been a regional centre with satellite communities on the surrounding hilltops of Winter Hill, Darwen Moor and Angelzarke Moor. As each year goes by, more and more sites come to light in these areas.

Stone circles to Turton & Entwistle Reservoir car park

Walk back to the white pole and turn right to follow old field boundary to its corner, overlooking Three Lowes. Cross the field on a left diagonal down to go over corner stile near ruin. Follow well-defined pathway on, between the Lowes, to go over fence stile. Follow fence down to roadway. Turn right and walk down the road to go left over a stile at footpath sign. Walk down to go over stile and on down to pass through green gate to walk down to the car park.

Car park to Whewell's Ruin

Follow the waterside track on, up into old Quarry, and on up to obtain magnificent views over the waters and Holcombe Moor. Walk on to the roadway. Cross the road then go left down the road to go over step-wall-stile 100 yards after road junction. Follow old field boundary up to go over fence stile and on up to go over stile in right-hand fence. Walk on following contour line to lone tree and farm ruin.

Whewell's

Whewell's is just another hillside ruin, remarkable only for its large bee-hive cellars. Above Whewell's are the moors of Turton and Longworth on whose tops are to be found several stone outcrops. The Hanging Stones, the Big Grey Stones and Andrews Buttery are huge arrangements of boulders, deeply scarred by the retreating ice of the glacier which deposited them there.

The Darwen Moor head   SD 675195

This large and grotesque stone head was found some years ago near the old mine shafts on Darwen Moor. Today it can be found on display in the Ribchester Roman Museum along with other so called 'Celtic' heads. Given the style of workmanship I doubt whether this head belongs to any of the early historical periods, and I feel that its origins must be sought in the Victorian period.

The survival of some of the true Celtic stone heads is linked mainly to the ancient cult of the severed head. To the Celts, in the head rested everything that made men what they are – it was the seat of the Celtic equivalent of the soul. Celtic warriors were head-hunters who kept the heads of their foes as trophies and Brigantian forts were adorned with human heads. Stone heads, not unlike the one found upon Darwen Moor, appear to have represented Celtic deities such as Maponus the northern god. Stone heads have been invested with special properties by local superstition, right up to the present day. Relics of an older paganism survive in many forms in modern Christianity; green men, imps, bearded ogres and whores adorn many of our local churches. The power of pagan superstition is long-lived and not easily set aside by reason.

THE DARWEN
MOOR HEAD

Whewell's to Hollinshead Hall

Leave the ruin by old gateposts to follow trackway on till it meets a well-rutted track. Turn left and walk up the new track and on up, passing old stone gate post and carry on towards the two mounds to go over fence stile. Follow right-hand fence, on past the mounds, to corner of fence. Follow path on to veer right at slight shale mound. Walk on over the moor to go over a cobble-lined stream onto pathway. Left, and follow pathway, passing 'seat', towards the 'pole'. On past the pole up to the signpost. (The Ribchester Stone Head was found over to your right). Follow the Belmont path down to pass through gate by ruin. Follow track down to where it meets trackway, right, and return to roadway and back to Hollinshead Hall.

Walk Three

Crucks and Castles

3, 4 or 7 miles. 2 or 4 hours

Use Map O.S. SD 61/71

A good starting point for all three walks is Rivington Lower Barn, having a good car park, toilets and refreshments. The longer walk leaves the Lower Barn to visit Rivington Village and Moses Cocker, then Rivington Hall Barn from where you can return to Lower Barn if you have only come for the short walk. We go on to climb up to the Pigeon Tower and Rivington Pike to return by way of Liverpool castle. The third walk again starts at Lower Barn to follow the avenue up to Rivington Hall Barn, there to link on to the larger walk which takes us up to the Pike. The choice is yours.

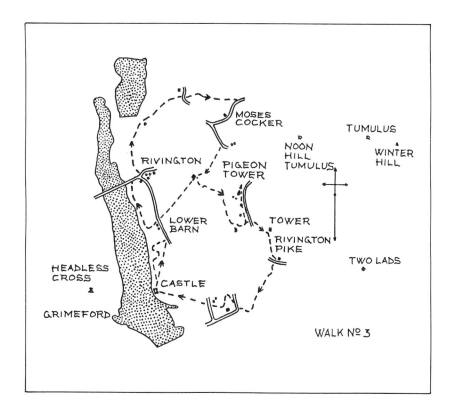

Great House Farm Barn

Great House Barn, referred to as Lower Barn, is constructed of large oak crucks, each side being taken from the same tree. This type of building frame has been used from the earliest times up until the late 17th century when the number of great oaks had declined almost to extinction. So widely had the great forests become depleted during this period that Charles I led a campaign to start a programme of re-forestation throughout the kingdom.

Lower Barn was built in the late 16th century and has been added to and rebuilt several times over the years. Today it houses an Information Centre for visitors to the West Pennine Moors and a small cafe. The adjacent stone building with mullioned windows was once Great House Farm. This has now been converted to provide a craft shop, rangers' office and public toilets.

Lower Barn to Rivington

On leaving Lower Barn walk past the car park to follow pathway along the side of the reservoir onto road. Turn right and walk up to Rivington church.

Rivington church and school

The first building of architectural interest one notices on approaching Rivington from the west is the school. It was rebuilt in 1714, on the site of the ancient free grammar school founded by Bishop Pilkington in 1566.

The church was first built around 1540, but only a few windows and the pulpit remain from that period. For the most part the church represents the rebuilding of around 1666. Inside is a monument to John Shawe, who died in 1627, in the form of a large brass plate with a skeleton on a mattress at the bottom.

Rivington Unitarian church

The Unitarian chapel was founded in 1662 and built in 1703, being one of the oldest of its kind in the country. It is built on a plain oblong plan with cross windows. The inside is furnished with box pews and the pulpit is in the middle of the north side. In the churchyard, by the gate, can be found a collection of decorated lintels from earlier houses of the district. The dates on the stones range from 1695 to 1732.

RIVINGTON CHAPEL CHURCHYARD

Rivington to Wilcock's Farm

On leaving the church turn right, walk past the stocks and cross the road to go through a kissing-gate. Follow path to go down the steps, over a stile and on, to go over another stile and through a kissing-gate. Walk along the lane to go over a stile. Follow right-hand fence to go over a stile. Follow path to go through a kissing-gate onto road. Turn left to walk up to Wilcock's Farm.

RIVINGTON CHAPEL CHURCHYARD

Wilcock's Farm

Wilcock's is a much altered and modernised 17th-century farmhouse. The ground floor is fairly intact to the left of the main doorway. The first floor level has been raised to hold a new slated roof. Above the doorway is a dated doorhead of 1670 with the initials R.I.E.

Wilcock's Farm to Moses Cocker's

Go over a stile by a gate on the side of the barn to go over next stile. Follow old trackway to go over a stile and on, to go over another stile. Follow left-hand fence, then wall, to turn right by a gate on the left. Follow track to go through a gate onto road. Turn right and walk on. Moses Cocker's is the first house on the right.

Moses Cocker's

Moses Cocker's is another attractive 17th-century farmhouse, the doorhead of which is dated 1693 with the initials C. R.A.M.

MOSES COCKER

Moses Cocker's to Rivington Hall Barn

Walk on along the road to T-junction. Turn left and walk on to turn right at the next lane. Follow lane to enter Rivington Hall Barn through a gate.

Rivington Hall Barn

This barn adjoins Rivington Hall, and is linked to Lower Barn by Hall Drive, a walk of about 5 minutes. The barn was originally used for agricultural purposes. During the winter months, livestock from nearby farms, together with their feed, were sheltered here. Later the barn was used solely as a hay store. Today the barn is used to host social functions and is a well known and loved landmark to the people of the surrounding district.

Rivington Hall

In the 17th century, Rivington Hall was the home of the Breres family. The initials of William Breres and his wife Martha appear on three of the building's datestones – 1694, 1700 and 1713. The hall was sold to John Andrews of Bolton in 1729, and his descendant, Robert Andrews, rebuilt the front of the hall in 1774.

RIVINGTON HALL

Rivington Hall Barn to Pigeon Tower

Walk up the lane on the left in front of the hall to turn left at fork. Walk on to go through a kissing-gate and on up the terraced path to Pigeon Tower.

Lord Leverhulme's moorland garden

The hillside gardens were laid out in 1905 by T. H. Mawson for Lord Leverhulme, a fervent advocate of landscape architecture. Upon this bleak hillside were built drives, terraces, lawns and water gardens. It is all now overgrown and in a state of natural decay. The bungalow, rebuilt after being burnt by suffragettes, has, like the lodges, been demolished by the Liverpool Corporation, but numerous garden buildings remain, the most prominent being the Dovecote Tower, contributing to a picturesque skyline. The ruins of several sets of loggias and terraces, and a bridge carrying a path over one of the drives, can also be made out.

To the north east of the Dovecote Tower lie the Bronze Age sites of Noon Hill and Winter Hill, and further north across the Yarrow Valley lies the kerbed mound of Standing Stone Hill.

Rivington Moor Bronze Age sites

Many Bronze Age sites are to be found on the moors around Winter Hill, and on the edge of the Rivington Moor plateau three substantial sites can easily be made out. To the south stands a cairn complex known as 'Two Lads'. On the west can be seen the Noon Hill tumulus, a disturbed round cairn with traces of a central burial. Some years ago an excavation found several secondary cremations, one being in an enlarged food vessel in a small stone cist. The latter, plus some barbed and tanged arrowheads found during the excavation, is on display in Bolton Museum. The third site is the composite cairn which stands near the summit of Winter Hill.

The Winter Hill tumulus was excavated in 1958 to determine the nature of its structure (the primary burial chamber had been robbed during an earlier excavation by 'treasure hunters') which was seen to be remarkably well-preserved. The diagram shows a plan of the cairn and a section at A-B. A kerb, 2 feet wide and approximately 18 inches high surrounded the mound. Inside this was a rising layer of subsoil, on the outer edges a large turf layer. These large sods, which formed

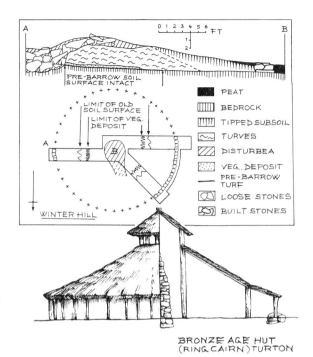

BRONZE AGE HUT
(RING CAIRN) TURTON

the inner part of the mound, were up to 3 feet across and in one case 9 inches thick and for the most part placed upside-down. Below this was a fibrous and matted layer of well-preserved vegetable matter, quite free from soil. In this compressed matter, remains of whinberry, ferns, cotton-grass, heather, mosses and birch-twigs, as well as an axe-cut piece of birch pole 3 inches in diameter and 20 inches long, were identifiable. The centre of the mound was seen to be a much disturbed cairn of stones.

The picture shows a possible reconstruction of what this type of structure would have looked like in its heyday: a turf-roofed round-house with a central stone hearth – smoke would escape through the turf cap-vent. The turfs would have been laid upside down, except for the topmost layer, to form an in-grown thatch effect. The vegetation layer represents the debris left behind when the hut was abandoned. The site can be placed in the local Early Bronze Age before the period of valley settlement.

For a better understanding of Bronze Age people the archaeologist would do well to study the living patterns and settlement of the North American Indians during the 17th and 18th century. For the general reader may I suggest Colin Renfrew's *Before Civilization* as being the best guide to the prehistoric periods in Europe.

Standing Stones Hill

Below Round Loaf, to the south east, at a height of 1,000 feet O.D., lies Standing Stones Hill. On its southerly edge can be found a kerbed mound with a stone retaining circle. It is this stone circle which gives the hill its name. The site appears to be intact and no archaeological investigations are recorded apart from the site location.

Pigeon Tower to Rivington Pike

Follow the road to turn left on the path leading up to the tower.

Rivington Pike Tower

The Pike Tower was built in 1733 by John Andrews to demonstrate, it is said, his ownership of the surrounding land. The tower was built on the site

of an ancient fire beacon. In an age before rapid communications, the lighting of a fire beacon on a prominent hill was a quick way of spreading news of national emergencies. Records show that the Pike beacon was lit on the night of July 19th 1588 to warn that the Spanish Armada had entered the English Channel. In recent years the Pike beacon has been lit to mark national celebrations; Queen Elizabeth's Silver Jubilee in 1977 and the Royal Wedding in 1981 being such occasions.

A fair has been held at the Pike for many years. Before 1900 it was held on Whit Sunday, but in 1900 it was changed to Good Friday. Since 1932 this has become an annual event attracting large numbers of visitors. The Good Friday Fair is followed on Easter Saturday by the Pike Race which attracts around 300 runners.

On a clear day excellent panoramic views of the surrounding area can be enjoyed from Rivington Pike. The Welsh mountains, the Isle of Man and the Cumbrian fells all come into view. The Bronze Age sites on Noon Hill, Winter Hill and Two Lads Hummock can also be made out from this point.

Rivington Pike to the castle

Go round the tower to walk down the path onto road to go through a gate opposite. Follow track down to go through a gate.

Walk down to junction to take the middle pathway. Walk on to turn left by a pond. Walk through the wood, veering left to Knowle House School. Follow the left-hand fence onto road, turn right and walk on to take path on the left to the castle.

The Liverpool Castle folly

On a small rise on the eastern shore of Lower Rivington Reservoir, known as Coblowe, stands a replica of the ruined Liverpool Castle. This was built by the soap manufacturer and industrialist W. H. Lever after he purchased the Rivington Hall estate in 1900 and turned much of it into Lever Park.

The re-creation of the ruin was started in 1912 using locally quarried stone, but finances were short and progress was slow and when Lever died in 1925 work on the project ceased altogether.

The original Liverpool Castle was built around 1235 by William de Ferrers, Earl of Derby. Between 1660 and 1685 the garrison was removed and the castle partly dismantled. The castle was finally demolished in 1725.

Restoration work on the castle replica is being carried out under the guidance of NWWA and should prove to be a useful attraction for visitors to the park.

Plan of the Liverpool Castle replica

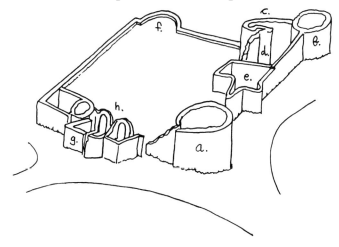

a) Great Tower; b) Castle Keep; c) Chapel;d) Great Hall; e) Kitchens; f) South-east Tower; g) Barbican & Outer Gate; h) Gatehouse

The castle to Lower Barn

Follow the path along the reservoir onto road. Follow the road to Lower Barn.

The Rivington Lower Barn head

This damaged stone head can be found on display inside Rivington Lower Barn. It was found by workmen during the excavations for the Yarrow Reservoir. Although referred to as a 'Celtic' head, its true origins are obscure. But given such ancient settlement in the area a pre-Conquest origin is more than probable.

The Headless Cross, Grimeford

The Headless Cross at Anderton can be found by the roadside at a cross roads on a minor road behind the Millstone Hotel on the A673. The cross and stocks are said to stand at the centre of the ancient village of Grimeford. The cross shaft is of an early, possibly 11th- or 10th-century, date. The legs of a figure, said to be those of St. Anthony, are on one face, and on the other is an X. The sides feature scroll and Greek key work respectively. In style, the cross resembles the Peel Fold 'Oldham's Cross' (now at Knowlemere Manor, Bowland). Mounted upon the ancient shafts is a flat sign-post stone pointing the way to Blegburn, Bolton, Wigan and Preston – the spelling for Blackburn is how it used to be pronounced in my youth.

Walk Four

Old homesteads around the Roman way

Allow 5 hours. 8 miles

Use Map O.S. 61/71

Many visitors to the area visit Turton Tower, and maybe Chapeltown or Jumbles Nature Trail; few stray further. This walk is designed to explore a few more of the area's ancient features. Jacobean farmsteads, ancient crosses, a Roman road and a possible Bronze Age burial mound will be featured, all set in an interesting landscape.

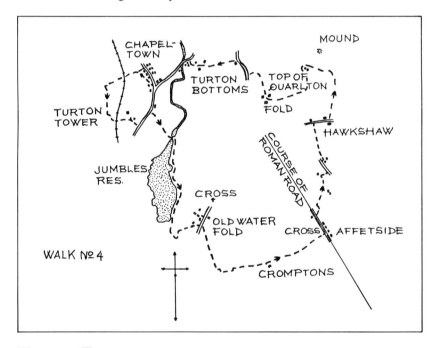

Turton Tower

The manor of Turton was a part of the barony of Manchester, assessed as one plough land in the earliest record. It was held chiefly by Richard de Lathom in 1212 as part of a knights fee. In 1302, it descended to the de Tarbocks, who were actually junior members of the Lathom family. With the death of John de Tarbock in 1420 the house and estate were left to his daughter Elizabeth, Tarbock in Merseyside being secured by the male heir. Elizabeth married William Orrell of Wigan and Turton became the seat of the Orrells. In 1596 a later William Orrell built the tower that we can, for the most part, still see today. By 1628 the Orrell family was in serious debt to a Manchester money lender and textile merchant, Humphrey Chetham,

who acquired the house. Chetham did not need Turton as a home and let the Orrells remain in residence until 1648. It remained in Chetham hands until it was sold to James Kay in 1835. The Kays restored the tower in grand Victorian style and enjoyed a lifestyle to match. In 1890 it was sold again, and again in 1903. Its last owner, Lady Nina Knowles, presented the tower to the Turton Urban District Council in 1930 and it became the Council Chamber. With local government re-organisation in 1974 Turton became part of the new borough of Blackburn and the tower is now a museum. The majority of the tower's contents came from the demolished Bradshaw Hall which stood nearby, bequeathed by the late Colonel Hardcastle.

The tower is an L-shaped building, originating in a pele tower, probably of the 15th century, with the remains of a spiral staircase in the north-east corner and an Elizabethan top storey. In 1596 the detached farmhouse was remodelled and attached to the pele, this work is partly timber-framed, partly of stone. The later ornate timbering is part of the work undertaken by Joseph Kay from 1835.

Turton Tower to Old Water Fold

Walk down the lane onto the road. Turn left and walk on to go over a stile by a gate on the right. Walk straight up to follow right-hand fence to go over a stile. Follow the path to go over a bridge. Turn right and walk along the path along the side of the reservoir. On past the Bird Reserve and Visitors Centre to beyond the reservoir dam, down the steps and through the small gateway. Right, and follow the path around the quarry and up to where the stream crosses the path. Turn left off the path and follow the small pathway above the quarry to go over stile. Walk on to go over stile by tree. Follow right-hand tree and hedge line to go through a gateway on the right before stile. Follow tree-line up to go over a stile onto roadway. Water Fold is on your left.

Water Fold

Water Fold is a small but substantial 17th-century farmhouse which stands overlooking Bradshaw Brook. The house retains all of its stone mullioned windows, each displaying hood-moulds above – a fine example of the area's vernacular architecture that will still be standing long after our modern edifices have returned to dust.

Old Water Fold to Affetside

Walk up the lane opposite Old Water Fold to go over a stile in corner where the lane bends. Follow left-hand hedgerow/fence to go over a stile. Walk straight on to cross a brook and on to go over a stile onto lane and over a stile opposite. Turn left and follow the iron-fence round to follow left-hand wall onto a lane. Walk up the lane and straight

on along the old track-way to go through a kissing-gate. Follow overhead lines to go through a gateway onto a path. Follow path into Affetside.

Affetside Cross

Affetside Cross stands upon the old Roman road between Manchester and Ribchester. The cross is said to mark the half-way point between London and Edinburgh. The Pack Horse Inn recalls a later use of the old Roman way. In centuries past, long lines of Galloway ponies would transport goods from the north-east Lancashire towns and villages to be traded in the great commercial centres of Manchester and Liverpool. Drovers' roads and trackways criss-cross the West Pennine Moors – a once vital network of communication and trade that today makes up the majority of footpaths used by walkers across the moors.

The Pack Horse Inn, Affetside

The Pack Horse was built in 1443 and some of the original timberwork and the ancient well from which water was drawn until recently (the Inn had no mains water supply) remain intact.

Above the fireplace in the old bar is the skull of George Whewell. It was Whewell who executed James the 7th Earl of Derby, in 1651.

John Bridge often frequented the inn until he was sentenced to death for counterfeiting in 1806. He was later reprieved and deported to Botany Bay, where his descendants today are amongst the wealthiest families in New South Wales.

The landlord is a very keen long distance walker, and you can always rely on a good welcome with an open fire and good food to set you up before the return leg.

Affetside to Hawkshaw

On leaving the Pack Horse Inn turn right and walk along the road (the road follows the course of the Roman road here) past cottages to turn right after the last house. Follow left-hand wall to go over a stone stile. Follow left-hand wall, then fence, to go over fence (by rights there should be a stile here). Cross field directly to go over next fence (a stile missing again). Follow left-hand fence to go through a gate. Turn right and walk down the lane onto road.

Turn left and walk on to turn right by the first house, then left to walk between animal sheds onto field. Follow left-hand fence to go through a gate. Follow left-hand fence to go over fence (a stile missing). Follow left-hand fence down to go through a gap in fences to cross a brook. Walk past the sheds onto road. Turn right and walk into Hawkshaw.

Hawkshaw to Top of Quarlton

Follow path opposite the Red Lion pub to go through a stile by gateway. Follow path to go over stile by gate. Walk along the trackway to go through stile by gate. Follow left-hand wall up to go over a stile. Follow field boundary (the tumulus is over on your right) to go over a stile by a gate on the left to enter Top of Quarlton.

Carve Hill tumulus

To the north east of Top of Quarlton stands Carve Hill upon the side of which stands a large steep-sided mound. The height of the mound on the west is 4.2 metres, and on the east 6.4 metres. Though there is no trace of a ditch, the mound is thought to have its origins in the Bronze Age and may be a large burial mound.

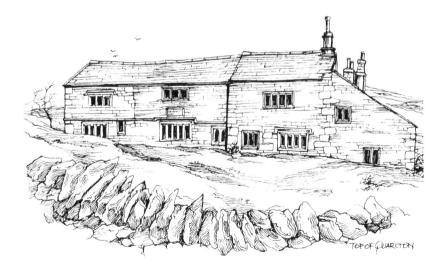

TOP OF QUARLTON

Quarlton

The hamlet of Quarlton is first mentioned in 1246 and the place-name is derived from the old German word 'quirn' meaning 'mill-stone'. The mining of mill-stones in the area is mentioned in 1332 and Quarlton probably formed the nucleus of the industry in the area at that time. The stone obtained from the moors above Edgworth is said to be one of the hardest grits in Britain, ideally suited for the manufacture of mill-stones.

During the 14th and 15th centuries, the manor of Quarlton was held by the Knights Hospitalers, of whom the local families of Radcliffe and Barton held land. In 1570 Andrew Barton paid 16d. for the Lordship of Quarlton; he seems to have got a better deal than the later Levers of Hulme, soap barons who craved such regal titles.

Top of Quarlton Farm has many styles of Jacobean architecture – round-headed stone windows stand side by side with the more common straight-headed mullions, and peculiar doorheads abound. I would dearly love to investigate this structure more fully. On viewing it I am sure that you will agree with me that this is a most interesting and inviting dwelling.

Top of Quarlton to Quarlton Fold

Enter yard gate and walk past the front of house, past the sheds into the field. Follow left-hand wall up to go over stile by gate onto trackway. Left, and walk down to the roadway. Right, to walk along the road to go over a stile in the fence on the right. Follow path through the wood to go over stile into field. Follow left-hand wall on down the field, veering right to go over stile in fence. Cross the field on a right diagonal to ruin. Walk down to enter Quarlton Fold.

Quarlton Fold

Quarlton Fold is a much altered 17th-century farmstead. A beam inside the barn is dated 1627 with the initials T.K.I.B.M. Above one of the barn's doorways is a dated doorhead of 1714 with the initials W.F.

Quarlton Fold to Chapeltown

Pass between side of farmhouse and barn to go through gate. Follow trackway on to field gate. Walk down the field on a right diagonal to go through a gate onto road. Turn right and walk along the road to go left down the driveway at the footpath sign after the first house. Walk down the drive and over the stile to follow right-hand wall, then fence to go over a stile and down the steps. Turn right then left and walk past the old factory to follow cobbled lane onto road. Turn left and walk on to turn right at junction. Walk up High Street to Chapeltown.

CHAPELTOWN
TURTON

Chapeltown

Chapeltown is an attractive moorland village of 17th- and 18th-century stone cottages. The main axis of the village is High Street with the Chetham Arms – an 18th-century inn – and the old stocks and cross at its northern end. The market cross marked the centre of Turton Fair, a well known and popular livestock fair held in the village until early this century. In 1885 the stocks and cross were moved to the grounds of Turton Tower. They were then renovated and brought back in the 1930s to stand in the Village Garden which was donated to the village by Miss Annie Barlow.

Chapeltown to Turton Tower

From the corner of the Chetham Arms walk down Kay Street and on along the cobbled lane to cross the railway. Go through kissing-gate at the corner of the house opposite. Follow left-hand wall up onto a lane. Turn left and walk along the lane to go through a kissing-gate. Take the lane on the left and walk down to go over a bridge to enter Turton Tower.

Walk Five

Oak Valley traverse

A circular walk encompassing the boundaries of the ancient Celtic settlement of Darwen – 10 miles 6 hours

Map: O.S. 2½" Sheet SD 62/72. Pathfinder Series

Darwen is a typical solid stone-hewn northern town, clearly an expression of the industrial age that spawned such places. The image it presents is that of the world of the late 19th century, but if one looks more closely, its former rural past can be discerned. Today, we walk through that former time before King Cotton ruled and explore a more pastoral Darwen.

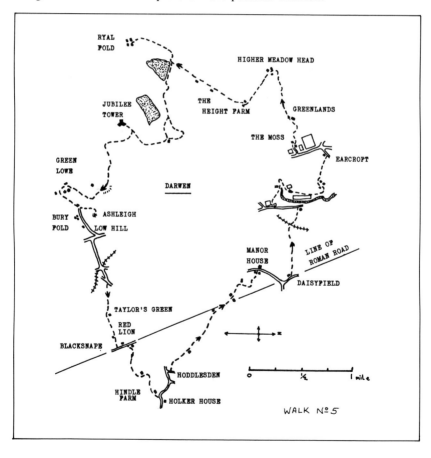

Moss Bridge to Moss Fold

Walk up Moss Fold Road and into Moss Fold. Enter farmyard by gateway and walk on up the track and past the Moss.

The Moss

Lower Moss is a grade III listed building, sadly going to rack and ruin at this moment in time. How unfortunate that such a fine 17th-century farmhouse

has today been relegated to the position of a mere junk store. The front of the house displays a flat-fronted porch with a wide off-set doorway and a tiny two-light mullioned window below the roof-line. All its ancient mullioned windows remain, though some are now bricked-up. The gable chimney is worthy of note, being one of the few examples in the area of original Jacobean moulded-edge type. To the rear is a gable projecting from the centre. The upper floor of the rear displays mullioned windows. It would be to Darwen's credit if this building could be restored, as Moss Fold, fronted by its running waters, could be a very attractive spot indeed.

Above Moss Fold stands the whitewashed farmstead of Greenlands. Close inspection of this hillside dwelling will reveal traces of its ancient mullioned windows. Look at the two odd windows to the left of the porch, and again high in the side gable.

Moss Fold to Higher Meadow Head Farm

Follow track on, around school playing-fields, to go over fence stile on the left. Cross field to go over stile onto trackway, past Greenlands farm, up to go over stile by green gate. Follow right-hand wall, over stile, and on to go over next stile. Follow right-hand hedge/fence to go over stile by gate. Walk on to the right of the farm and go over stile into farmyard. Walk around the barn, turn left up the track and walk on to Higher Meadow Head.

Higher Meadow Head Farm, Tockholes   SD 670238

The farmstead comprises a ruined 17th-century farmhouse, barn and shippon of the 19th century and a 20th-century farmhouse.

The shippon, which appears at one time to have doubled as a hen house, has a flight of 'fox' steps leading to the first floor; these are situated in the outside gable. The farmer is of the opinion that the barn used to be an inn standing on the route that coaches took travelling between Belthorn, Tockholes and Feniscowles in the 18th and 19th centuries. It seems unlikely that the present building served this purpose as it appeared to be a late-Victorian purpose built barn. However, the first O.S. map of the 1840s does not appear to show this building but a smaller one in a slightly different position, so this one could conceivably have been the inn.

The ruined farmhouse has unfortunately had its date-stone stolen but the farmer recollects it as being 1688, the same as Earcroft Barn. The building is constructed of stone and appears to have been built in two stages and styles. The only complete wall still standing is the west-facing gable which has at ground floor level a small round-headed window of a 17th-century date. At the first floor is a square window of more modern appearance. There is no roof to the building and the remaining walls are in various states of collapse with an assortment of old and modern outbuildings attached. The west side of the main building appears to have been built as a separate house, there being large corner stones both at the gable end and five yards down each longitudinal wall, possibly at one time forming another gable. The east side contrasts with this in only having large corner stones where it meets the gable, suggesting that it is a very early extension.

The south-facing wall on the west side has a four-light mullioned window on the ground floor with some ⅜ ins. thick glass in position. To the left of this is a doorway. On the east side of this wall, at ground floor level, is a two-light mullioned window and next to it a filled-in doorway or window with a 90 ins. label mould. At the first floor is a small square window.

The north wall has two out-buildings up against it, obscuring a number of features. At the west side at ground floor level is a relatively modern window and at first floor level there are traces of a filled-in window and a wooden beam in the wall. Behind the outbuildings a four-light mullioned window with large label mould can be picked out, with a door adjacent to it. Almost immediately to the left of this is what appears to be an older doorway with dressed corner stones from the east gable coming into the left side of it. Behind this, inside the building, is an odd-looking wall parallel with the doorway. On the first floor is a three-light mullioned window. The east gable is almost totally obscured by brick outbuildings.

Higher Meadow Head to Jubilee Tower

Pass through farmyard, between old stone hen-house and farmhouse, through gate and on up through next gate. Follow right-hand fence on, over stile, to enter Height farmyard by way of stile on side of barn. Walk down to lower whitewashed cottage then right to follow path onto golf course. Follow left-hand wall down to corner then cross the golf course on a right diagonal, past ruin, to go over stile and walk on to farm track. Left through gate, then right to follow roadway (notice the old grindstone set into the wall, a memorial to Abella Duxbury) to reservoir. Left along the side of the reservoir and then follow track up, over cattle grid, and on to Water Board house. Take the right fork and follow track up to top fork. Bear left along old grassed trackway to go over stile into walled trackway. Follow track up to tower.

Jubilee Tower

The eighty-six foot high Darwen Tower, as it is locally known, was erected in 1898 to mark the Jubilee of Queen Victoria. The tower dominates the skyline for miles around and provides a vantage point from which the surrounding countryside can be viewed. The edifice stands on the summit of Beacon Hill, named after the ancient signal beacon that once stood here. The fire-beacon would be lit to commemorate an event or Saint's day and sometimes to signal approaching danger or as a rallying sign for the local militia.

Jubilee Tower to Green Lowe Farm

Walk out of the tower to the triangulation point. Take the right-hand path down, then right again at cross-paths. Follow wide track down, through gate, and on down to pass through green iron gate. Up the right-hand bank and over stile. Follow path up to beneath cables. Walk on the old tramway banking for twelve paces then left to follow track down to pass over stile. Follow right-hand fence to pass over corner stile. Walk down the track (notice India Mill chimney on your left) past rubbish tip entrance and on down to just before gateway (this is the site of an old farmstead, the farm well is set into the banking on the right). Go over the fence on your right and walk directly across the field in the direction of Green Lowe Farm set in the trees, over fences (should be stiles here) and on to the right of the farm (the mounds can be seen over on your left). Enter farmyard and walk down farm track to junction (notice the weavers windows on the ground floor of the farmhouse).

Green Lowe to Bury Fold

Turn left at the junction and walk down lane, past cottages, onto roadway and down to Bury Fold, 100 yards down on the right.

Bury Fold

Bury Fold takes its name from the Burry family who lived here between 1520 and 1850. William Berre was assessed for lands in Darwen in 1523. In

1672, another William Berry, a Nonconformist, had the house at Bury Fold licensed as a preaching place. The Nonconformist doctrine spread many strong roots in the Darwen area among a people who have always had an independent attitude towards life.

The farmhouse at Bury Fold is now divided into three dwellings, yet this does not detract from it being a very imposing structure, retaining its own ancient individual character, this being mainly due to the high standard of restoration carried out by its owners. The house's dominant feature is its massive central multi-storey porch with projecting upper-walls. The off-set doorway displays a deeply cut ogee doorhead above which is a datestone of 1673 with the arms of the Burry family. The first-floor porch window has an ogee head and hood mould, and above this is a two-light round-headed mullioned window. All in all a very pleasing edifice.

Bronze Age ring-bank burial mound, Ashleigh St, Darwen

No physical evidence remains of Darwen's only known barrow, it having been destroyed during October 1864 as excavations were being made for the foundations of Ashleigh House, which incidentally was itself demolished during 1986.

Contemporary reports about its excavation state that it was of circular form about 30 yards in diameter, being formed on a naze or promontory of an undulating plateau overlooking the Darwen Valley. Its height was said to vary from 10 to 12 feet on the east side and between 2 or 3 feet on the west, the

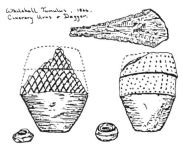

centre being about 6 feet in diameter and consisting of a slight hollow. Ten interments appear to have been made, one being just a heap of burnt bones, the others, having been enclosed in urns, the majority of which are badly broken, consisted of ashes and fragments of bone together with unrecognisable pieces of bronze. Two urns also contained 'incense cups' and another a 7½″ bronze knife or dagger.

The design of the urns is similar to those from the Middle Bronze Age (1200/1500 B.C.). All but two of the urns were found within an area 21 ft by 14 ft, whilst one was 40 feet away. They were, with one exception, placed in the earth with the oriface pointing upwards and were covered with slabs, the depth at which they were found varying from 1 to 2 feet.

Many superstitions were attached to the barrow and its destruction in the 1860s, with the country people speaking of the place being haunted by 'boggarts' and children having been known to take off their clogs or shoes and walk past it barefoot in the night time.

An excavation which took place in 1986 found only evidence of the original lie of the land, the naze apparently having been levelled during the construction of the house.

For over ninety years the Whitehall Urns have been on display in the Reference Library at Darwen – safe, but still accessible to the public. Some time ago the urns were taken by the County Archaeologist, Ben Edwards, to be restored by Lancashire Museums Service. This work has now been done and the urns are due to be returned to the Reference Library at Darwen.

Two other possible Bronze Age sites

Two mounds stand to the east across from Green Lowe Farm. The meadow in which they stand is used for grazing and the mounds have not been excavated. The name 'lowe' is often an indication of a burial mound, and the mounds at Green Lowe do not appear to be natural formations. Given the field evidence, a survey of this possible site is called for.

Bury Fold to Low Hill House

Return to roadway and walk down to Low Hill House on the right.

Low Hill House

Low Hill House was built in 1812 and was, until 1817, the home of Samuel Crompton, inventor of the spinning mule. The east and west wings were added later by Eccles Shorrock. Crompton's spinning mule is on display in Lewis Textile Museum, Blackburn.

LOW HILL HOUSE
BUILT 1812
THE HOME UNTIL 1817 OF
SAMUEL CROMPTON
INVENTOR OF THE SPINNINGMULE
THE EAST AND WEST WINGS
WERE ADDED LATER BY
ECCLES SHORROCK

Low Hill House to Red Lion Inn, Blacksnape

Walk down to the main road, turn right, then left down Grimshaw Street and on up over railway bridge and crossroads into Pole Lane. Walk on to the bend to fork right up the farm track. Walk up to Taylor's Green entrance to go over stile by the wall on the right. Follow wall up, over stiles, onto Roman road. Turn left and walk down to the Red Lion Inn.

Roman road, Blacksnape

This principal line of communications and supply between the Roman forts of Manchester (Mamueium) and Ribchester (Bremetennacum) was probably first constructed during the governorship of Agricola. Like other military roads of the 1st century, it cut across important river valley routes allowing the rapid deployment of troops in the event of the Pennine tribes showing signs of aggressive activity. Cross communications were also essential to the efficiency of the system, and both Manchester and Ribchester were joined by trans-Pennine roads to York.

A few years ago, during alterations to the cellar of the Red Lion Inn, a section of the Roman road was exposed showing several periods of construction and the paved upper surface.

Red Lion to Hindle Farm

Walk down from the inn to turn right at footpath sign by white cottage. Walk up the track to go over stile on the right by footpath sign. Cross field following left-hand fence to go over fence stile.

Cross the field directly to far corner, through gateway to follow left-hand fence to corner. Over the fence (should be a stile here) and follow fence left to trackway. Turn left and walk on past Stand Farm into housing estate. Walk along the roadway keeping right, down Chapman Road to go right at first turning. Walk on down to go over stile by gate on left. Follow fence and old wall down, over stile to stream. Cross the stream to enter old trackway by stile. Walk up the trackway to Hindle Farm.

Hindle Farm to Holker House

Follow lane on to the road and walk up to Holker House, on the left.

Holker House

Holker House is an old messuage standing at the upper end of the hamlet of Hoddlesden. The front of the house is symmetrical, having plain mullioned windows on the ground floor and stepped round-headed ones on the upper floor. The central porch has a wide doorway with drip moulding above. Above the first floor porch window is a date tablet of 1691 with the initials R.E.I. and a lion rampant. The initials are possibly Entwistle of Entwistle, builders of the house.

HOLKER HOUSE

In 1751 Christopher and Alice Hindle owned Holker House. The Hindle family also owned Langshaw Head which they restored in 1799. The property of Langshaw Head dates back to the 13th century and stands on what is locally named the Saxon road. The Saxon road or 'Limmers Gate' was a major pack horse route from West Lancashire to the east of England. The pack horses were referred to as 'Lime Gals' (Galloway Ponies). Lime was 'imported' and coal was 'exported' to and from Hoddlesden. This road enters the village area by Heys Lane, through Stacks Cottage, Langshaw Head and on through Pickup Bank.

Holker House to Ranken Arms, Hoddlesden

Walk back down the road and into the village of Hoddlesden. The Ranken Arms is up on the left.

Hoddlesden

Hoddlesden is first mentioned in 1296 as then being a stock raising area belonging to Henry de Lacy. In the 1340s Adam de Holden and Adam Grimshaw are recorded as having paid for land and waste land in Hoddlesden. By the 16th century there was a hall in Hoddlesden and the Ranken Arms now stands on the

HODDLESDEN

site of this earlier dwelling of the Marsden family.

The picture shows Queen's Square, where numbers 2 and 4 were hand-loom weavers' cottages, the work being carried out in the cellar. Number 6 used to be a farmhouse. It has small mullioned windows on the ground floor with dripstones. The barns to this farm stood where the war memorial is now.

Outside the Ranken Arms stands a large mill-stone positioned in the cobbled forecourt. This had been lying on the river bank outside Lower Darwen Paper Mill until recently when it was cleaned and suitably engraved to form a permanent memorial in the village.

Ranken Arms to Manor House

Walk down Bayne Street to turn first left into Kings Drive. Walk on to Dukes Drive, turn left and follow round onto trackway between houses, up the steps and over the stile. Follow right-hand fence to corner and go over fence (should be a stile here) to follow left-hand fence to near barn. Pass through field gate on the left, turn right and walk on to pass through red field gate onto farm lane. Walk on into narrow field opposite, and on to where it narrows at meeting of fences (should be a stile here). Go over fence to stile and follow right-hand old wall and fence along to corner. Go over fence (should be a stile here) and walk over disturbed ground to trackway. Cross trackway and on to pass through gateway. Cross the field directly towards farm to pass over stile in wall. Follow right-hand fence, past the barn, and onto trackway. Walk up to the farm. Passing the front of the farm walk on directly to pass over stile in far wall. Follow right-hand fence into Harwood Fold. Pass through iron farm gate (notice the old cheese press weight on the right) and walk down the track to Shaw Fold. At Shaw Fold go through gates on the right and walk down track to old bath horse trough on the left. Pass through gap at rear of trough and walk down the field to hedgerow. Over stile, turn left and walk on to go through old stone gate posts and onto the Handels Arms (painted white). Enter roadway by gate, turn right and walk down to Manor House on the left.

Manor House, Eccleshill

The ancient site of the Manor House of Eccleshill is said to be the old farm at Waterfoot. The present building is a solid looking yeoman farmhouse with many mullioned windows. Above the front door is a dated doorhead of 1697, with the initials E.A.K. To the right of the front door is an ancient cross base holding the head of an old cross. Whitaker in his *History of Whalley* states that 'a stone cross two feet high, with some Roman coins under it, was found in Eccleshill near Guide, upon the property of Mr. Hodgson of Clerkenhill'. He argues that Christian missionaries engraved the cross on a

Roman milestone. Folklore tells of the Manor House cross being the grave marker of a Christian Roman soldier, buried by the side of the Roman road. Perhaps further research will determine the true nature of this tiny cross. Several Roman objects have been found in the area, the most interesting being a beautiful and

MANOR HOUSE perfect fibula (brooch/safety pin) of bronze which was discovered in the grounds of Harwood Fold in March, 1834.

The place-name Eccleshill means 'the church hill'. This Celtic word is derived from a British form of the Latin word 'ecclesia' and implies the existence of some sort of Celtic population centre with organized worship. In Lancashire we have five possible Romano-British Christian sites, Eccleshill in Blackburnshire being one of them. Blackburnshire was organised on a Celtic territorial model − a central *caput* (Whalley) between two *commotes,* each divided into multiple estates of two *vills,* arable land and summer pasture. Eccleshill with Mellor was one such multiple estate, Mellor being the estate lands and Eccleshill the upland pasture. Apart from the name we have no other firm evidence that an early church stood at Eccleshill, in fact no archaeological evidence is at present available for any of the 'eccles' sites. Was Eccleshill the 'church hill', or was it the upland pasture, the 'church hill' being Mellor? There is a tradition in the village of Mellor that a church, now said to be buried, stood on the top of Mellor Moor by the ancient earthwork. This area is known locally as 'Sod Huts'. Recent aerial photography shows what could be a rampart and other structures near the earthwork. Also, according to Prior Wessington of Durham (1416), the body of St Cuthbert was rested at Mellor and a chapel was dedicated to the saint.

Manor House to Daisyfield

Walk down the road, left past the Johnson Road turning on to Daisyfield, the first farm on the left.

Daisyfield

Daisyfield, formerly called Davey Field, is an early 18th-century farmhouse of some character. The gabled porch has a dated doorhead of 1723, and the ground floor displays a fine row of mullioned windows with a running drip-mould above.

DAISYFIELD

On the walk between Daisyfield and Earcroft is a wooden fence stile, the step of which is the weight of an old cheese press.

Daisyfield stands in an area known as Grimshaw, a place-name that suggests that way back in the mists of time this was once an haunted grove.

Daisyfield to Earcroft

Go over the roadside wall stile at the corner of the barn. Pass through field gate and follow right-hand hedge till just after it bends to the right, then cross the field on a slight left diagonal to a stile in a hollow near where three fences meet (notice the stone step of the stile, it is the weight of an old cheese press). Over stile and follow right-hand fence along, over stile, over next stile to follow left-hand fence to corner. Walk on across the old brickworks to go under railway bridge in between the industrial building on the left and the pylon on the right. Walk on to farm, over stile and through farmyard onto the road. Turn left and walk up the road to turn right up a track after the first building (Crown Paints) on the right. Follow track on down, over the river Darwen and on to junction. Turn left and walk on up to the roadway. Turn right and walk on to warehouse. Take the path by the right corner of the warehouse.

Through the ginnel then follow right-hand wall, over stile and on, under fence and on to go over stile. Follow right-hand wall on down the hill to go over stile. Follow left-hand fence to farm track. Walk on through the farmyard and into the lane. Walk up the lane to bend to go over stile on the right. Follow right-hand hedge to stream. Cross the stream and go over stile. Walk up the hill to the right of the pylon, over two stiles onto Sandy Lane. Earcroft is the farm on the left.

Earcroft

A farm site consisting of 18/19th-century farm houses with attached barn, granary store, a shippon and 30m west a 17th-century barn.

Until recently, the farmhouse had in its front wall a small mullioned window over the door and remnants of it suggest that it was much older than the present building and possibly came from an earlier 17th-century building. The barn attached to the house also contains in its south wall sections of stone very similar to that found in the 17th-century barn.

The granary store, in front of the farmhouse, has two ground floor doors and one window; on the upper floor one door, reached by a flight of ten external stone steps of substantial proportions. There are two windows, one being very small. The roof is covered in stone flag. This type of building is rare in the area.

The shippon appears to have its full complement of fittings and feels warm and cosy and, in stark contrast to many modern ones, it too has a stone flag roof.

The 17th-century barn is dated 1688 on a door lintel on the east wall, the date is in relief with the initials H.P.C.P. above it. The doorway has now been converted into a window. Near the apex of the wall is a small circular window. Construction of the barn is in coursed sandstone with quoins and a stone flag roof. On one of the projecting bays there is a wagon entrance with a porch roof carried on a moulded double corbel to the right.

This is a long walk, but I think you will agree, a greatly rewarding one full of contrast and interest. Given a limit on time, or some other factor, the walk may be divided into two halves — Darwen Moor and the Blacksnape/Eccleshill area, using the good bus service to return to base.

Walk Six

Livesey-cum-Tockholes

A circular walk from the Royal Arms at Tockholes. 8 miles, 5 hours

Map: O.S. 2½" sheet SD 62/72. Pathfinder Series

Set in hidden rural splendour on Blackburn's south-western boundary can be found the ancient manor of Livesey-cum-Tockholes. Rationalised farming hardly seems to have affected the area. Old trackways of an earlier coaching age can still be discerned and many old 16th-century houses and farmsteads still stand proud, all recalling the charm of a former rural age. Tockholes is and always will be an enigma, with its stories of treacle mines, of the flight of Prince Rupert against Cromwell's might, of ancient stones and coaching roads. Nothing is recorded but much is recalled by local families who claim descent from Toca, a legendary figure whose story is lost to the mists of time. The walk takes in ten sites of historical and architectural interest through a landscape which will remain in one's mind forever.

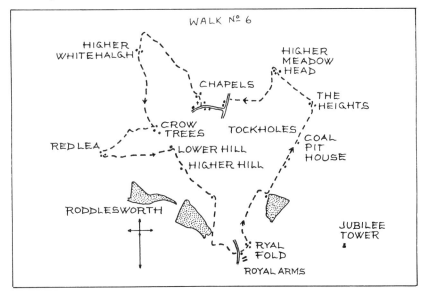

The Royal Arms

The Royal Arms makes a good starting point, with easy access to car parking and bus stops, along with genial hospitality, good ale and very reasonably priced lunches served in most rustic surroundings, all add up to a day out to remember.

Royal Arms to Ryal Fold

Walk down the lane at the side of the pub to enter Ryal Fold.

Ryal Fold

Ryal Fold is a small group of farmhouses and cottages which date from the 17th century, situated at the foot of Tockholes Moor and Earndale Reservoir. As is recorded on the date-stone, the yeoman farmhouse pictured here was built for John and Elizabeth Walmsley in 1676. The owners of an earlier house on the site were the Marsdens. Hugh Marsden of Ryal is recorded as having paid the King's Subsidy Tax in 1523, and William Marsden was a governor of Blackburn Grammar School in 1634.

The house has an interesting design with a fine gabled porch. Here we see a round-headed main entrance doorway, above which the three-light mullioned window has round-headed lights, and above this is a single round-headed window set in the gable. An incongruous lean-to has been built onto the front, which ought to be removed if the house is to be returned to its ancient splendour. The barn standing opposite the house is one of the finest examples of watershot stone walling in this part of Lancashire. Indeed, so well is the stone cut that one could almost walk up the wall sides.

Another house at Ryal has been recently modernised to a large degree, but still shows some of the early 17th-century mullioned windows with hood-moulds.

Ryal Fold to Berry's Tenement Farm

Pass through the gate at the end of the farmyard and walk down the track to go through a gate. Follow right-hand wall, then fence down and on up, following right-hand hedgerow to go through a gate in wall. Turn right and follow path down to edge of reservoir to go left over a cattle grid. Walk along the lane to enter Berry's Farm.

Berry's Tenement Farm

Built into a wall near the farmhouse is an old millstone. Inscribed upon its face is the following: 'IN MEMORY OF ABELLA WIFE OF DUXBURY'

Berry's Tenement Farm to the Heights

Walk up alongside a farmshed to go through a gate. Turn right and walk past the shed to follow right-hand wall to go over a stile by a gate. Walk along the track, past the ruin on the right, to walk up the golf course on a left diagonal to go through a gate in a wall. Follow right-hand wall, then fence, to go over a stile. Walk directly down to go through a gate into the Height Farm.

The Heights to Higher Meadow Head

Go between a small white cottage and a farmshed to go through a gate. Walk past the cottage to follow left-hand wall down to go over an old fence (there should be a stile here). Walk straight down to enter Higher Meadow Head through two gateways.

(A description of Meadow Head can be found in Walk 5).

Higher Meadow Head to Chapels Farm

Walk past the house to turn left after the ruin. Follow old trackway to join a lane and on along the lane onto road. Turn left and walk on to turn right by a public house. Walk down the lane to turn right by a churchyard. Follow lane into Chapels Farm.

CHAPELS FARM, TOCHOLES

Chapels Farm and old well

Standing on the opposite side to the church is the 17th-century building of Chapels Farm.

A little way up the lane, to the east of the church, stands a castellated roadside well. An inscribed stone inside the well's round-headed arch informs

us that 'The Norman arch over this well was removed from Gerstane Hall, Tockholes, (Gerstane or Garstang Hall stood before its demolition near to the Royal Arms Hotel at Ryal) and placed here in 1910 by the Rev. A. T. Cornfield'. Beneath the inscription is an heraldic shield with the Latin scroll 'Serva Fidem'. Even in my youth the community at Tockholes was still served by local wells for the supply of water. One I remember well stands opposite the Bull Inn, but with all the chemicals used on the land today I could not recommend its usage. Near to the Bull Inn there once stood an ancient cross, said to have been mutilated by Roundhead soldiers during the Civil Wars. On the same roadway as Chapels Well can be found an old doorhead, now used as a wall gate lintel, with a date 1692 and the initials R.A., displayed within an ogee framework.

St Stephen's School and Church

The church was built between 1831-33, and today only the front of the south porch has been preserved. It now leads to a modern church building of 1965. Propped up against the church walls are a number of decorated stone slabs bearing heraldic designs.

The prized possession of the churchyard is the ancient Toches Stone. Its plinth, a retooled cheese-press weight, is inscribed and informs us — 'The upper portion of this monument is supposed to be a remnant of the old Parish Preaching Cross probably dating from 984. The lower portion is probably a part of the ancient Toches Stone from which the parish took its name'.

The place-name of Tockholes is Old English and means 'Tocca's Valley', Tocca being an old Saxon personal name going back to the 8th century.

St Stephen's School was erected in 1854 upon the glebe land by voluntary subscription, aided by a grant from the National Society in London. The open-air pulpit, built of window mullions, is of around 1900-10, replacing an earlier wooden one from Mellor Church.

TOCHES STONE

All in all St Stephen's churchyard presents the strangest variety of church buildings and sculpture I have ever seen, all adding to the mystery and folklore of Tockholes.

Chapels Farm to Higher Whitehalgh

Walk through the farmyard to go over a stile by a gate and over a stile opposite. Cross field on a slight right diagonal to go over a stile by a gate. Follow left-hand hedgerow to go over a stile. Follow path down to go over a footbridge and through a gate opposite. Follow left-hand wall to go over a stile. Follow left-hand wall to go over next stile onto lane. Turn left and follow the lane into Higher Whitehalgh.

Higher Whitehalgh

The ivy all but hides the fine 17th-century farmhouse of Higher Whitehalgh. The asymmetrical north-west frontage holds a fine selection of mullioned windows. The off-centre gabled porch has a datestone above the upper floor window, 1616, with the initials of the builder Thomas Livesey, along with the initials G.MR.S.

Whitehalgh was given in the time of Edward I, by William, son of Henry de Livesey, to Richard his brother for a yearly rent of two shillings. During the reign of Edward II a William Livesey adopted Whitehalgh as his surname. The Livesey family claim to have lived on the site since they first built a dwelling here in 940 and, given that they are one of the oldest families in Lancashire, this may well be so.

Higher Whitehalgh 1616

Many folk tales have grown up around Whitehalgh. The most noted is that Oliver Cromwell is said to have stayed three nights in the house, during which time he and his men fought the Battle of Darwen Moor. The story goes that the three hundred men who died in the battle are buried in the sandy field facing the house. Cromwell is supposed to have spoken words over them from an open pulpit built into the gable-end of the house. Locals point to the hood-mouldings set in the gable as being all that remains of the pulpit.

Another story tells of the true Lancashire witches, a tiny people of only four feet in height, who were fervently non-Catholic. These tiny Celts served the local farmers by acting as animal healers, using wild herbs and ancient skills now lost. It was through their efforts and skill that Lancashire was supposed to have bred such prized cattle and horses. The Catholics thought their work to be that of the Devil and hunted down the tiny folk. During such times of persecution, farms such as Whitehalgh offered refuge within their walls. These secret passageways, I am informed, are still in existence in the walls today.

Higher Whitehalgh to Crow Trees

Pass front of the house and go over stile by gate. On a right diagonal walk down the field to go over gap wall stile near sheds. Follow path through wood to go over footbridge (notice old gate post in stream). Follow left-hand fence for 350 yards to go left, over stream by way of footbridge. Walk up the field to go over stile near left-hand electrical cable post. Walk up the field to old gate posts, walk on to go over fence stile on the right. Follow left-hand fence on, over footbridge and on to farm lane, right, and on to Crow Trees.

Higher and Lower Crow Trees

Higher Crow Trees is a much altered 17th-century house. Remains of the old mullioned windows and hood moulds can still be made out. To the right of the lean-to doorway is a small round-headed window above which are the initials I.M., being those of John Marsden of Tockholes.

The field opposite Crow Trees is known as Kill or Pit Field. It was here in 1833 that thirty eight horses' heads, various bones and a number of cannon balls were dug up. The finds were said to be the relics of a battle fought nearby in around 1642 during the Civil War. Once again we find a claim for the Battle of Darwen Moor, though in this part of Tockholes they claim that the dead are buried in the old Tockholes churchyard, which was demolished in 1832.

Lower Crow Trees is another 17th-century house, the mullioned windows with drip-mouldings presenting a fine frontage. Above a doorway on the barn opposite is an inscribed stone bearing the initials W.M., and the date 1671.

The house is said to be an old coaching house and stables. In fact Lower Crow Trees stands on the fork of two ancient trackways. Both are metalled, one we shall follow round to Red Lea Farm and the other we have partly walked along coming up from Higher Whitehalgh. Remember the gate posts in the stream by the footbridge? The road is said to be the old coaching road between Bolton and Clitheroe.

Crow Trees to Red Lea

On past Lower Crow Trees and through the iron field gate. Follow left-hand fence along and down to ford and gate. Pass through gate and follow left-hand fence on to Red Lea.

Red Lea

Red Lea is an old hamlet which stands above the River Roddlesworth, secluded by woods on its western side and which contains a small number of 17th-century buildings. The best preserved of these is Red Lea Farm, a solid stone-built house with many interesting features. Mullioned windows complete with hood-moulds add charm to the asymmetrical frontage. The gabled storeyed porch has an off-centre doorway, and above the drip-moulding a framed date tablet is set in the stonework. It bears the initials of Richard and Elizabeth (or Ellen) Aspden and the date 1674.

A branch of the Hoghton family of Hoghton Tower lived at Red Lea during the 16th and 17th centuries. William Hoghton, second son of Richard Hoghton of Tockholes, appears in the records in 1602, and died at Red Lea in 1623. When Elizabeth Hoghton married Richard Aspden the house of Red Lea was rebuilt for them. Inside is a large Inglenook fireplace and a priest's hiding hole. Richard was a trustee in a deed of gift to Tockholes Chapel in 1670 and one Thomas Aspden of Red Lea was a trustee of the Nonconformist Meeting House in 1735.

Red Lea to Lower Hill Manor House

Walk past the front of Red Lea Farm to rear of house to go over stile. Follow old trackway to go over slab-bridge and stile on the left, follow fence to go over next stile. Walk up the field on a left diagonal to old marl pit. Walk around on right of pit and on to old gate posts. Follow trackway to Manor House.

Lower Hill Manor House

The large 17th-century building of Lower Hill, formerly known as the Manor House, has now been converted into four cottages. Along with the odd sized gables and built-on extensions the house presents a very distorted frontage. Happily all the original features remain and with a little thought and co-operation Lower Hill could easily be restored to its former glory. One feature that has been restored by one of the tenants is a small window overlooking the valley. In those dark days when the Roman Faith was outlawed, a lamp would be lit and placed in the window as a signal to the local populace that a priest was about to hold a secret Mass. Adam Richardson is recorded to have lived at Lower Hill in 1735. It was his second son Ralph who built the Silk Hall in 1764.

Manor House to Higher Hill

From the front of Manor House walk up to go through gated wall stile. Follow wall up to Higher Hill.

Higher Hill

Higher Hill is by far the most outstanding house in Tockholes. It was built by Ralph Walmsley in 1612. His initials and the date are inscribed upon a small round-headed window on the north face of the house. Ralph died on the 22nd November, 1665, at the age of 100 years, and is buried in Blackburn churchyard (now the Cathedral grounds).

Roger de Walmerslegh was living in an earlier house on the site in 1334, and from a branch of his family descended the notable families of Walmsley of Showley Hall and Walmsley of Dunkenhalgh.

The gabled porch is a very solid looking structure. Above the doorway, where one would usually expect to find the stone date tablet, is a carved head surrounded by mouldings. Above is a three-light mullioned window with hood mouldings above. Set in the gable is a round-headed niche, perhaps for holding a figure. Another niche can be found on the ground floor of the south-wing gable-end. Below the valley of the south wall is a medieval latrine set on corbels; inside, the wooden seat still exists – so look up with care.

To the south of Higher Hill lies the wooded valley of the River Roddlesworth. A nature trail has been made through the wood and starts at the Royal Arms Hotel; details and a map can be found on a notice board near the pub.

Higher Hill to the Royal Arms

Go over stile near 'dog sign' and follow right-hand wall to go over stile and down house driveway. Left across the grass and over wall stile. Walk down the field on a right diagonal to go over fence stile into wood. On the same diagonal follow woodland path on, over ravine, over stream to go over next stream, here follow path up to the road opposite the Royal Arms. Walk down the lane at the side of the pub on to Ryal Fold.

The Royal Arms makes a good stop for lunch, good ale and food are served daily in most genial surroundings.

Other walking books from Carnegie Press

Historic Walks around Bleasdale, by John Dixon and Jaana Jarvinen, (ISBN 0 948789 18 2), price £2.75. This relatively unspoilt and quiet area of Lancashire is explored in four walks, which can be split up in various ways. The area is steeped in beautiful countryside and fascinating history.

Historic Walks around Ribchester, by John Dixon and Jaana Jarvinen, (ISBN 0 948789 19 0), price £2.75. Ribchester is well known for its Roman past. But less well known are the lovely, peaceful and very interesting nooks and corners described in this book.

Historic Walks around the Hodder Valley, by John Dixon and Jaana Jarvinen, (ISBN 0 948789 22 0), price £2.75. A beautiful addition to the series, due to be published in August 1988.

Walking from Garstang, by Ian Brodie (ISBN 0 948789 03 4), price £2.25. A very popular book covering a lovely part of Lancashire.

You can order any of these books from your local bookshop or newsagent. Alternatively, write to the publishers, Carnegie Press, 125 Woodplumpton Road, Cadley, Preston PR2 2LS for any book or an up to date catalogue. We also stock a wide range of books on local history and interest.